Move Like A Pro

How to Help Kids Throw Faster, Hit Harder, and Run Quicker for the Long Term Dream.

By

Christopher Romano M.A., CSCS*D, RSCC

Detroit Tigers Minor League Strength & Conditioning Coach

&

Joseph Lee Romano

Table of Contents

This book is dedicated to the awesome Hopewell Baseball coaches that coach my son's baseball team. They do youth baseball the right way. With the vast majority of my time being spent coaching with the Detroit Tigers, without these guys, my son wouldn't be able to be playing ball. Knowing he is in good hands allows me to focus on my job and not worry that he is going to get hurt.

Preface

The goal for this book is to help provide quality information and ideas for youth baseball coaches and parents of youth baseball players. There is a lot of information out there, some great, some totally wrong. I truly believe that everyone volunteering their time to coach kids in any sport has only the best of intentions. Most youth coaches are parents of the players, who have regular jobs, and did not go to school with the intention of being a coach. Much of how they coach is based on how they were coached when they were kids. I'm 41 years old at the time of this book. When I was in little league, it was the late 1980s through the early 1990s. Exercise Science was not an actual career field, let alone a degree program at major universities. Over the past 25-30 years, science and research have really come a long way. Money has been invested in researching the best ways to train for specific sports, starting with the elite athletes and trickling down to youth athletes. Ideas that were considered wrong back in the 1980s have since been proven to actually be correct.

One such idea is the fact that adolescents can and should be participating in resistance training. Building off research from researchers like Dr. Avery Faigenbaum, national organizations, such as the National Strength & Conditioning Association, National Academy of Sports Medicine, The American Academy of Pediatrics, as well as many others, have posted position statements and articles supporting children participating in resistance training. In fact, The American Academy of Pediatrics recommends resistance training for children under proper supervision in its June 2020 issue of *Pediatrics.* In that it states "Misconceptions about children and resistance-training are refuted by research that shows benefits of strength-building, including injury prevention and overall fitness". In case you are confused, resistance training IS strength training.

Now, one key takeaway from what the experts conducting this research all say is that resistance training is beneficial for children **under qualified supervision**. Qualified is the key word here. Your neighbor who likes to lift weights, or your son's best friend's dad who used to be a body builder and is now an insurance salesman do not count as 'qualified'. The fitness influencer that has 10 million followers on Instagram and keeps posting photos of their abs is not 'qualified'. And (here is where I may get myself into trouble), your son's PE teacher or school coach may or may not be 'qualified'. That would depend on their degree and prior experience. At one point, I wanted to be a PE teacher in order to coach strength & conditioning at my old high school. I took the state of Georgia GACE text for a provisional teaching license in PE. Nothing on that exam was even in the furthest stretch related to resistance/strength training or strength & conditioning. The majority of it was on basic health and the rules of games like four square. With that said, a lot of PE teachers have gone beyond the state requirements and taken classes or gotten degrees in exercise science. My point of including PE teachers in this is simply that the ones who got a bachelors in elementary education and then went into PE would be considered not 'qualified' to supervise a child doing a strength program, while the teacher who has a degree in physiology and got certified to teach PE would be plenty qualified. Later in in this book I explain the difference between a personal trainer and a Strength & Conditioning coach, using the example of a general practice doctor and an orthopedist as a more common analogy, so here I will explain the difference between a PE teacher and a Strength & Conditioning coach. PE teachers are a critical part of a child's physical development. They are educated and knowledgeable in active games kids can play, and teach the kids to be physically active. They also teach the kids how to play multiple sports and games. Using the medical world analogy, they would be the equivalent of your pediatrician. PE teachers are experts on general child fitness and health. However, would you go to a pediatrician to operate on your child's broken arm? Of course not! You would go to a orthopedist (maybe even a more specialized pediatric orthopedist). You would do this because the orthopedist is educated in the specific area your child requires help in, just as you should seek out a Strength & Conditioning Coach (maybe even one who specializes in training children – if you have one in your area) to help develop your child for athletic success.

Speaking of personal trainers, I would also recommend being careful about just going to your local fitness center / gym and hiring a personal trainer to work with your child. Many of them are educated in general fitness, and do not understand specifically what your child needs. Specifically, the later chapters regarding beneficial and not so beneficial exercises would be a topic that some personal trainers may have trouble with, which we will cover later in this book. When you are spending your money on training, and when you're talking about your child, you want to ensure you are getting the most benefit for the time you and your child are investing. So something like ladder drills would not be nearly as beneficial as doing wall marches, for example (all discussed and explained later on in this book).

So, when hiring a coach to work with your child, two key terms to look for would be: "Degree in Exercise Science/physiology/biomechanics/ or anything similar", "CSCS" or "Certified Strength & Conditioning Specialist". You can find great coaches without these; however, someone who has either or both of these would be someone more likely to provide a better quality program for your child, as they have been exposed to the science side of strength training, as opposed to being someone who just likes to go to the gym and wants to train people.

If you have any questions or comments regarding what I talked about here, please feel free to reach out to me; I am always happy to help youth coaches. I check my Twitter messages daily, so that is the easiest way to reach me, @CoachCris_.

Chapter 1: Why is Strength & Conditioning Important for Children?

So why am I writing a book focused on teaching youth baseball players the fundamentals of strength & conditioning? Well, for starters, as a strength and conditioning professional, and a dad to two youth baseball players, I see a big void in actual knowledge in this area. Currently, I am a Strength Coach in the Detroit Tigers organization, but I have also been a Strength & Conditioning coach at a large 7A high school in Georgia, as well as a junior varsity pitching coach, and 5U, 6U, 7U, and 14U baseball coach. This is a topic I have been invited to speak on at national conventions, such as the American Baseball Coaches Association (ABCA). While I train professional baseball players for a living, setting the foundation for our kids is near and dear to my heart. Through my role with the Detroit Tigers, I have had the benefit to spend a lot of time in the Dominican Republic, working with our Latin American players, and have seen the differences in movements between them and the American players. My 8 year old son also got the opportunity to play on the San Pedro de Macoris 10-12 year old team in the Dominican this past summer, so I also have an advantage to see how those children train compared to American kids. The differences in the development of the Latin American players versus our kids shows in their movement patterns as they get older.

For example, when doing movement screenings on 18-25 year old professional baseball players, the biggest differences I have noticed are in the squat and lunge patterns. A lot of this is going to be due to the fact that American kids grow up wearing running shoes, while the Latin kids grow up wearing flat shoes or spending a lot of time barefoot. When screening their movement patterns, the Latin kids have much stronger ankle stability, but the American kids perform a lunge pattern better. Using proper exercises that develop both muscular strength and joint stability is the types of exercises we will discuss later in this book. The goal here would be to have both ankle stability and be able to perform the lunge pattern well.

The other two topics that I will cover in this book were actually the idea of my 8 year old (Lee). He has seen me train the high schoolers, and has seen how I train him, which raises questions when we arrive early or stay late from his practices and he sees what some other kids are doing. So, as someone who has a lot of experience in this particular field, I want to help spread some basic knowledge that youth parents and coaches can use with their kids. With that said, we will talk about age-appropriate exercises for youth (elementary – middle school), as well as some common exercises that aren't ideal, all with the goal of creating a sound base of movement to set the kids up for success over the long run.

However, one thing that I feel is super important to point out before we get into the main content of this book is what the goal of strength & conditioning is, and what it needs to be for this age group. Because of the name, strength & conditioning, most people think the goal is to create stronger and better conditioned athletes, which is actually not the primary goal, especially while working with youth athletes. At the professional level, the main goal of the strength coach is to help prepare the players to endure the long season, by providing them with the tools necessary to not only do their job successfully, but to remain healthy over the course of the season. During the off season is when we can really focus on developing strength and power. During the pre-season and in season, we just want to make sure we are giving the players what they need in order to keep them healthy and on the field. At the youth level, it is a little different. For the elementary age kids, the vast majority of their strength increases will come just from growing. As much as we would like to believe a good strength program will get the child stronger and develop their muscles, but that just isn't the case. Once they hit puberty in middle school/high school, you can help them develop strength & power in the weight room. For the elementary age kids, the goal needs to be developing and teaching good movement. When a child moves well, they will appear stronger because they may be able to lift heavier objects, throw harder, or swing harder, but that is the result of efficient and proper movement, not developing more muscle fiber.

There are two main reasons to teach proper movement at a young age. First, the majority of injuries that occur at older ages, such as high school, college, or pro come from poor movement. So, training the brain and muscles to have proper movement patterns early on will help the athlete lower injury risk as they grow up. The second reason is not as important, but still valuable. Teaching proper movement patterns early on helps start the athlete's training age, so when they hit puberty, they have the proper movement patterns down, and can start benefitting from strength training right away. Children that have not been exposed to proper movement patterns must first learn them. As an example, it takes a long time for some athletes to learn to squat properly (we will address the squat pattern later in the book). So, consider my son Lee, who has been squatting since he was 4 years old, versus a future high school teammate that has never had any training prior to getting to high school. Which boy has an advantage? They may both be 14 years old, but the one that has been doing it for 10 years has a major head start. This is something that factors in when comparing the movement levels and injury risks of the Latin players versus the American players. Having a head start of even a year or two is a big advantage over the long run.

Chapter 2: What Exercises Should My Youth Baseball Player Be Doing?

Let's start this topic by addressing a decades old myth about youth and weight training. As supported by numerous peer reviewed studies, led by Dr. Avery Faigenbaum's 1999 paper, "The effects of different resistance training protocols on muscular strength & endurance development in children" shows that when supervised by a <u>qualified</u> professional, strength & conditioning is safe, and beneficial to the youth athlete. Now, the term qualified is subjective for the most part. As we talked about earlier, the dad volunteering to coach the team and having the kids do exercises because they're the same exercises he did when he played high school ball is not a qualified professional. The dad who reads this book, and decides to have his kids max out their back squat, is not a qualified professional. The certified personal trainer at the gym down the street may or may not be a qualified professional in this context. Surely they have experience in the fitness world, but Strength & Conditioning is a specialty off of general fitness. Think about it in the context of doctors. All doctors have an understanding of how the body works. Your general practice/ family practice doctor would be the fitness world's equivalent to a Certified Personal Trainer. For your everyday adult wanting to get exercise and maybe lose a few pounds, the personal trainer would be suitable. However, if you need some specific medical attention, such as shoulder surgery, you would seek out an orthopedist, since they are the expert in that specific field. In the fitness world dealing with athletes, this would be where a Strength & Conditioning coach comes into play. Someone with a degree in exercise science, or a related field, and/or who has the NSCA Certified Strength & Conditioning Specialist certification is more than likely a qualified professional. I know we already covered this earlier, but I feel it is important enough to mention twice. When seeking a trainer for your kids, the keys to look for are the coach's education, certification, and experience. Obviously, like any profession, just having letters after your name is not a guarantee of being good at the job; it just helps the likelihood of them knowing what they're doing. So with that said, I am 100% in favor of children using weights, as long as it is with a qualified coach/trainer.

However, weight training is not the focus of this book. My goal for this book is to provide the regular dad / volunteer little league coach with some quality knowledge that they can use to benefit their kids. If you are interested in learning more about weight training, you can check out my other recently released book, "The Book on Olympic Lifts and Their Role in Sports Performance".

For the rest of this chapter, I'm going to provide exercises you can use at practice with your kids, using minimal equipment, as well as the rationale/benefit of each exercise. How you decide to pair them, and which ones you choose to use or not use, is totally up to you. These are all basic movements that when done correctly, will build a base of solid foundational movement, and apply to the sport of baseball. There are other movements that are excellent for developing movement patterns, but aren't as beneficial for baseball. Given the limited field time most little league teams get, I want to focus on the movements that are most relevant to the sport of baseball (although I am a big supporter of every kid playing multiple sports).

Squat:

Key points to teaching the squat:

1: Feet set up should be hip to shoulder width apart with the toes turned slightly out.

2: When squatting, the knees should track in line with the feet. If the knees are inside the feet, it is a valgus position (valgus basically means the knees are collapsing inwards), and this puts strain on the ligaments within the knee joint. If this happens, this would be the time to use the "knees out" or "pretend you have a beach ball between your legs" queue.

3: The heels MUST stay in contact with the floor the entire time. If the heel comes off the floor and the athlete goes on the balls of his feet, it needs to be corrected ASAP. Biomechanically, a weight shift onto the front of the foot will cause strain on the lower back due to the body having to compensate to stay balanced. It could be that the set up/foot width needs to be adjusted, or he may have poor ankle mobility. Poor ankle mobility would put him at a greater risk of injury as well as have a potential negative impact in on the field performance. For example, an infielder with greater ankle mobility may have an easier time fielding a ball in the hole. One way you can check this is to elevate his heels slightly on a raised surface and see if that corrects the issue. If it does, then you need to work on his ankle mobility (several drills can be found on YouTube). Since elementary school aged children move around enough while playing, ankle mobility should not be an issue. For older kids, high school and college age, ankle mobility would need to be looked at more carefully in this scenario.

4: We want the athlete to squat to a depth below parallel, but not to a point where they lose core stability. You will notice this when their torso starts to collapse forward, and their back rounds. A child squatting should be able to get their hips below the plane of the top of the knee while maintaining their torso upright.

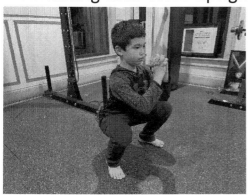

5: It is okay, and actually a good thing, if the knees go over the toes. This happens in baseball as well as in life, so do not fall victim to the old myth of the knees cannot pass over the toes in a squat.

6: If holding a weight, such as a medicine ball, kettlebell, or dumbbell, it should be in contact with the chest, with the elbows in, and not flared out.

Lunge:

Key points to the lunge:

1: When lunging, whether it is forwards or backwards, the stepping motion should be straight. What I mean by this is the stepping foot should not go in front or behind the planted foot, nor should it finish wider than it was in a standing position.

2: At the bottom of the lunge, both knees should be flexed at 90 degree angles.

3: The torso should be upright.

Rear Foot Elevated Squat:

Keys to the RFE Squat:

1: The torso should remain upright the whole time.

2: The front foot should be placed at a point that when squatting, the femur (the bone between the knee and hip) will be parallel to the floor at the bottom of the movement.

3: Knees must be pointing straight forward.

4: When ascending from the bottom, the athlete should be able to push hard into the floor with the front foot.

5: If holding a weight, such as a medicine ball, kettlebell, or dumbbell, it should be in contact with the chest, with the elbows in, and not flared out.

Push-Up

Keys to the Pushup:

This is one that I see done incorrectly by my own kids, as well as their friends, quite often.

1: The way I teach the most efficient and safest way to perform a pushup is to have the athlete lay face down on the floor. While lying face down, ask them to raise their chest as high as they can without using their hands. Then place their hands even with the point at which the torso loses contact with the floor, and then slide the hands out to the side about one inch. This will place their hands at the proper and most efficient point for doing a pushup (or a bench press for older kids).

2: One very important part of a pushup for the safety of a baseball player is elbow positioning. The elbows should never go out further than a 45 degree angle. Yes, with the elbows in, most kids will say it is harder, but keeping the elbows in reduces the stress placed on the shoulder. It is also a more powerful position. Think about if you're going to shove someone. Would you have your elbows out or in?

3: The fingers on each hand should be spread as wide as possible, providing a stable base of support. The thumb joint should form a 90 degree angle like an "L" with the thumbs perpendicular to the athlete's torso.

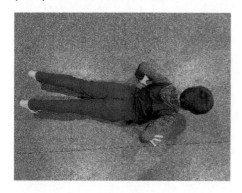

4: The hardest part of the pushup when coaching young athletes is to ensure the entire body raises all at one time. There should be no arching of the back, or piking of the hips, as shown below.

Pike   Arch

Plank:

For this age group, I prefer the front plank over side planks. I want to make sure the movements are as basic as can be, so they're done safely and effectively. While a side plank is an excellent exercise for older baseball players, at the elementary age and middle school age groups, I feel more comfortable not adding potential extra stress to their shoulders and elbows.

Keys to the front plank.

1: It's a plank, so you should be able to draw a straight line from the top of the heels to the head. The length of time the kids can perform this will vary, and it is important to have them stop the plank when they can no longer maintain form. Remember that it is about development at this age. Teaching proper neurological patterns (muscle memory) is what we are looking for, so trying to teach mental toughness by fighting through holding a poorly performed plank is counterproductive. The elbows should not be flared out.

Medicine Ball Throw:

There are multiple versions of the medicine ball throw. With this age group you can start in a batting stance, kneeling on the floor, or back to the target. If you notice, in these photos Lee is using a basketball instead of a weighted medicine ball. Since he is 8 years old, I feel the basketball is more appropriate in this case. As the exercise becomes easy for him, I will move over to a weighted medicine ball. The key to this exercise is to throw the ball hard, and most 8 years olds will have trouble throwing a 6-8LB medicine ball hard. So you will need to use your judgement on what kind of ball to use here. With that said, the exercise is called the medicine ball throw, regardless of what ball we are using.

Keys to the MB Throw:

1: Regardless of the starting position, you want to be sure the athlete is having all of their momentum going towards the target. One good queue for this is to say "the side of the lead hip needs to move towards the target". The rest of the body will follow the lead hip.

Medicine Ball Slam:

Keys to the MB Slam:

1: Starting position should be on tip toes, arms fully extended over the head.

2: The athlete should flex at the hips and knees as they perform the downward movement.

3: The ball should land directly in front of their feet.

Medicine Ball Fake Scoop:

This is one that I rarely see kids doing, yet it is very important in creating longevity in healthy players. It trains the deceleration portion of a rotation movement, such as a batter swinging.

Keys to the MB Fake Scoop:

1: Start with the medicine ball at the side of the hips, both hands on the ball.

2: Rotate the hips, as you raise the ball to finish over the opposite shoulder from the hip you started on, performing a scooping motion.

3: The athlete does not let go of the ball.

4: Youth athletes at the elementary school age will not be able to use a heavy ball. I use a basketball with my 8 year old when he does the MB Fake Scoop.

Jump Squat:

Keys to the Jump Squat:

1: Start with the feet between hip and shoulder width.

2: The heels need to stay in contact with the floor on the descending portion of the squat movement.

3: At the peak of the jump, the hips and ankles should be in full extension, with the arms fully extended overhead.

Kettlebell/Dumbbell Swing:

This is one of the weighted movements I want to include in this book, mainly because it has high value for baseball players, but is often done incorrectly. I want to emphasize starting out with a light weight on this exercise. It takes some athletes longer than others to get the kettlebell movement pattern down, and it is always safe to use an extra light weight when learning a new movement pattern.

In this case, the lightest kettlebells I have at my home are 16LB, which are way too heavy to have a 5 year old like Alex use, so we used a lighter dumbbell instead. This is also a good time to point out the fact that there are generally multiple options of equipment that can be used to get the same result.

Keys to the KB Swing:

1: The set up position should be with the feet shoulder width apart, both hands on the kettlebell, and elbows fully extended. The athlete should start with the KB on the floor, so the hips will be bent, similar to the position a football center would snap the ball from. The back needs to be flat in this position.

2: The initial movement is pulling the kettlebell backwards into the hips as the athlete begins to stand upright. This would be almost identical to a football center snapping the football. The kettlebell should swing back, almost touching the bottom of the glutes.

3: The athlete will then extend the hips as fast as he can, generating speed on the kettlebell only by using the glutes and hamstrings. The arms should never do the lifting in a kettlebell swing. The arms are only there acting as a pendulum.

4: This part is extremely important for baseball players. The kettlebell should not go any higher than shoulder height. If the kettlebell goes above that, say to overhead, the position the shoulders compresses the joint, adding un-necessary strain, and risking a shoulder impingement. Therefore, if you are going to have your players do kettlebell swings, it is imperative to ensure they do not bring the hands higher than shoulder height.

5: The kettlebell swing is a hip hinge pattern. The knees should not bend into a squatting pattern. In fact, the knees should not move much, if at all, during a kettlebell swing. They should remain slightly bent the entire time. Please reference earlier in this chapter to see a squat pattern and compare it with the hinge pattern pictured below.

6: The heels should never leave contact with the floor during this entire exercise.

7: This is a movement that I would not suggest introducing until at least 10 years old. You'll have some kids that can get the pattern down at a younger age, but that would be on a case by case basis. By age 10, I feel most kids in a team setting would be able to understand the coaching queues enough to safely do this movement.

Farmers Carries/ High Low Carries / Suitcase Carries:

These are awesome exercises I would encourage everyone to do. They build grip strength and core strength.

Keys to a Farmers Carry:

This exercise uses two weights, one in each hand. The athlete should have both arms to their side with the weights near the side of the legs. The shoulders need to be set back and down, and not in a shrugged position.

Keys to a Suitcase Carry:

This exercise uses one weight, and is otherwise performed exactly as the farmers carry. The key to this exercise is to ensure the athlete is not rotating at the hips, or leaning to one side too much. They should be using core strength to maintain as upright as possible.

Keys to a High Low Carry:

This exercise uses two weights and is performed very similarly to the previous two. The difference here is one weight is held exactly the same way as in the suitcase carry, while the other is simultaneously held on the shoulder. The weight on the shoulder should be resting on the side of the bent arm holding it, with the elbow no further out than about 45 degrees.

90/90 shin box

This exercise is very helpful in developing proper movement of the hip joints.

Keys to the 90/90 Shin Box:

1: The athlete starts sitting down, with both knees bent at 90 degrees and facing the same direction. The athlete then rotates both hips, raising the knees up and over to facing the other side.

2: It is acceptable for athletes learning this movement to have their hands on the ground behind them.

3: The more advanced version of this drill is to raise the hips off the floor, and into extension at the end of each repetition.

Glute Bridge:

The exercise is very good for developing and maintaining hip extension at a young age, and can be used with weights as they get older to develop power.

Keys to the Glute Bridge:

1: Laying on the ground, face up, and feet flat on the floor, the athlete pushes into the floor through the feet to raise the hips as high as possible.

2: The more advanced version of the Glute Bridge would be the Single Leg Glute Bridge.

Wall March:

This is an acceleration drill, teaching the athletes to apply more force into the ground when they run. If you break down the actual movement demands of the sport of baseball you will notice the most common way an athlete moves is by accelerating / increasing their speed.

Let's look at a couple examples of common baseball situations. For the sake of this example, let's use a professional baseball field with 90' base paths as our field. Sprinting as fast as possible, a player will not hit full speed at any point of base running. The common base running plays would be:

1) Sprinting 90' in a straight line running from home to 1st base

2) Sprinting less than 90 feet – after taking a lead – when stealing a base
3) Sprinting on a curve while running multiple bases, such as a batter hitting a double, triple, or inside the park home run, or even a runner going from 1st to 3rd on a batted ball.

It takes roughly 30 yards / 90' for elite 100 yard sprinters to hit their maximum speed, and they train to hit that speed for their sport. Therefore, it is safe to say that baseball players, even the greats, are not going to hit top speed running to 1st base. Therefore they are constantly accelerating / increasing their rate of speed. If 90' is not enough room to hit top speed, then they also will not hit top speed stealing a base.

The multi-base scenarios all involve special circumstances, such as sprinting in a curved pattern, having to quickly slow down to stop AT a target (the base), or having to step on a target (the base), mid stride, while sprinting on a curve. All of these factors also make it nearly impossible to hit top speed. In fact, it has been shown that average base runners actually slow down while rounding a base because they have to change their stride to step on the base and then accelerate again going to the next base.

Now, you may be thinking to yourself, "Ok Chris, maybe base running is mostly acceleration but what about fielding?" Yes, there could be a few scenarios where a corner outfielder has to sprint more than 90' to track down a fly ball hit into the gap or into the corner. However, the vast majority of balls they have to track down would be hit less than 90' away from their position, therefore rendering training to maintain top sprint speed much less valuable than training for faster acceleration.

Since we have now established acceleration as being a highly important part of baseball, let's look at one of the best ways to train to accelerate faster.

Keys to the Wall March:

1: Lean into the wall at a 45-degree angle, with arms extended parallel to the ground and palms pressing into the wall.

2: Raise one knee up as high as possible, with toes pointing as high as possible.

3: Strike the ground hard with the foot that was raised, and alternate legs.

4: Perform 4-5 foot strikes with each leg in a running pattern, with each repetition starting with one knee up as high as possible.

Anti-Rotation Squat

For this exercise, you will tie a low-level resistance band to a fence post, or squat rack, or anything similar. The athlete will hold the band out in front with the arms fully extended, while standing to the side of the post. The athlete needs to fight the band that is trying to turn the chest to face the post. While working against the band's pull, the athlete will squat, not allowing the band to affect their torso position.

Keys to the Anti-Rotation Squat:

1: The athlete stands in the same squat stance described earlier in this chapter. The difference is they hold their arms extended and parallel to the floor with their hands holding the resistance band at chest height.

2: Athlete performs the squat as described earlier in this chapter, while fighting against the pull of the band.

Pallof Press

There are many versions of the Pallof Press: split stance, parallel stance, walking, etc. However, for this age group, I will only address the parallel stance since it is the most basic variation to teach and learn. Like the Anti-Rotation Squat and the MB Fake Scoop, the Pallof Press serves as an anti-rotational exercise.

Keys to the Pallof Press:

1: The athlete sets their feet in the same position as the Anti-Rotation Squat, parallel to each other, and under the hips.

2: The athlete hinges (bends) at the hips, with the knees unlocked, and the chest between a 45-degree angle from the floor and parallel to the floor.

3: The athlete starts by holding the band by the chest, and then presses outward to extend the elbows. To complete the repetition, he will return the hands to the chest.

Step Ups

The Step Up is a basic unilateral strength exercise. Unilateral exercises work on training one side of the body at a time. You will need a box or step. This can be done with or without weights.

Keys to the Step Up:

1: The highest the box or step should be would be when the athlete has one foot flat on top of the box/step, the knee is bent to a 90 degree angle.

2: The athlete pushes into the box/step to bring the rest of the body up and at the top of the repetition both feet should be flat on top of the box.

3: The athlete then steps back with the leg that was originally on the ground to complete the repetition.

Wall Angel

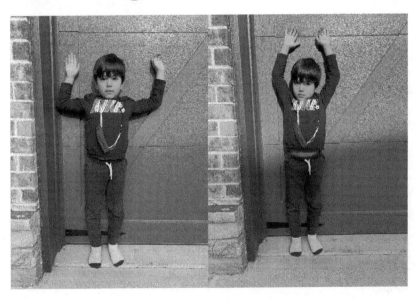

This is a mobility exercise, which is very important for baseball players. The goal is to increase the range of motion of the shoulder.

Keys to the Wall Angel:

1: Athlete stands with the heels, glutes, shoulders, back of the head, elbows, and back of the hand touching the wall.

2: The athlete starts the repetition with the elbows bent 90 degrees, and the triceps parallel to the floor.

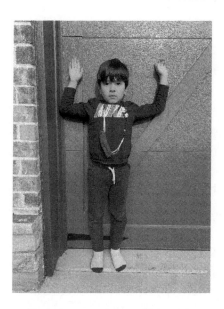

3: Maintaining all body parts mentioned in step 1 touching the wall, the athlete raises their arms along the wall to the maximum height possible. If any of the mentioned body parts leaves contact with the wall, they went too far. The athlete then lowers the arms back to the starting position to complete the repetition.

4: This movement needs to be done slowly to get the full benefit.

Chapter 3: Exercises that provide little benefit:

There is a lot I could write about in this chapter. In fact, I am sure most knowledgeable coaches could probably write an entire book on stuff not to do. Instead of using this platform to go off on a discussion of opinions on certain exercises, I would rather use it to talk about some exercises coaches use during their limited time/space with their athletes that, let's just say, would be lower on the best bang for your buck scale, than the exercises in the previous chapter, and provide a sound, sometimes scientific, rationale behind my statements.

The number one thing that I see youth (elementary school age) baseball coaches have their players do is conditioning. Anyone who spends any amount of time around children this age will know they run around and play a LOT. In the course of any given Saturday afternoon, or even any average after school afternoon, my kids are outside playing soccer, shooting basketballs, playing all sports golf battle, riding bikes, jumping on the trampoline, playing at the pool, etc. Believe me, kids ages 5-12 have a solid aerobic base. Now, factor in the sport of baseball is 95% or more an anaerobic sport, why are we having our kids running poles? The 10-15 minutes after practice that is often spent running poles (jogging from foul pole to foul pole along the warning track) could be much better used working on movement skills, going over hitting approaches, talking about throwing mechanics, etc. Or better yet, working on speed development!

Speaking of speed development, this is the number one deficiency I see in youth sports. Teaching proper sprinting mechanics is not easy, and often a professional coach is really needed to work with kids on the proper sprinting mechanics. I am not going to get into that here as plenty of awesome books have been written about that topic (one I HIGHLY recommend is <u>The Science of Speed, The Art of Sprint</u> by Tom Tellez and Carl Lewis). What I want to discuss here is HOW speed training should be incorporated to replace aerobic conditioning for youth baseball players.

First off, speed work is absolutely not the same as conditioning. If you are sprinting 30 yards and resting 10 seconds between sprints, that is aerobic conditioning, not speed work. There is only one way to sprint faster, not factoring in improvements in running form. That way is applying more force into the ground with each foot plant. To apply maximum force, you must be fully rested. No one should be on the ground tired, or worse yet, throwing up after a speed training session. So, my suggestion is that if you want to work on improving your players' speed, go read Tellez's book and supplement your practices with the techniques and drills he lists in there, as opposed to wasting time at the end of practice having the kids run mindless and unproductive poles. (A disclaimer here: at older ages, there would be appropriate times to develop an aerobic base; it just isn't necessary for younger baseball players).

Number 2: do your best to avoid falling into the trap of "back when I played, we did it this way". Times have changed since we (if you're reading this book you're most likely a dad and close to my age) were kids. Entire college degrees, master's degrees, and doctorates are offered now specifically looking at sports performance and exercise science. The amount of knowledge we have today vs the 1980s and 1990s is an entire world greater. With that said, several of the exercises that used to be used in baseball when we were growing up, have since been shown either ineffective (running poles), or even counterproductive (speed ladders).

Speaking of speed ladders, they're a very controversial topic among the fitness world. Social media influencers love to show them, as well as all sorts of circus tricks like the athlete balancing on a bosu ball while squatting with one kettlebell overhead, but let's take a look at what benefit and counter benefit speed/agility ladders actually have. As I stated earlier, to run faster, you have to apply more force into the floor. But speed ladder drills train the exact opposite of that. The ladder trains quick feet, less ground contact time, and short choppy strides. Think for a second here, does training quick feet, short ground contact time, and short choppy strides sound anything like applying greater force into the ground? Absolutely not! Watch some video of Ricky Henderson stealing bases. He is doing the exact opposite of that. Speed ladders also force you into an upright position. But look at any good base runner. Are they ever in an upright positon with the feet under them? No! They're accelerating, which puts their entire body at a forward leaning angle, which is impossible to train using a speed ladder.

Let's consider the demands of the sport of baseball. Most of the running done in baseball is acceleration, not top end speed. During acceleration, your body is leaning forward, and you are pushing hard into the ground to move faster. So, in this case, would it be more beneficial to do speed ladder drills or a wall march?

Okay, so now we can agree, the ladder drills don't help us run faster, and could reinforce poor sprinting mechanics. What about using the ladder for agility work? Nope, that is not a benefit of the ladder either. If you look up the definition of agility in any exercise science textbook, you will find something along the lines of 'the ability to react or change direction quickly in response to an outside stimulus'. In a baseball context, being agile would be reacting to a bad hop, or adjusting to catch a bad throw that ricochets off a baserunner. Doing a pre-planned foot pattern in the speed ladder is not agility work at all. So, would doing 'agility' drills with the ladder be more beneficial than say, working on positional footwork or some specific short hop drills during practice? If you really want to do agility drills, then I suggest using some reactive drills that also incorporate agility. One way I do this with the professional baseball players is I have them move in a direction on command. For example, I move my arm to the right and they side shuffle to the right. They react to what I do. That is agility.

With that said, by no means am I suggesting to throw away your speed ladder. For youth athletes, it has a lot of potential benefit; you just need to use it correctly. For the youth athlete, that would be teaching them lower body coordination and change of direction drills. An example of a coordination drill I like that my son does with his team is the moving sideways quick in and out footwork drill on the ladder. Moving the body sideways, while the feet go front and back quickly, is teaching lower body coordination. In baseball, most of the change in direction patterns we see are side to side, so doing side to side drills with the ladder can help develop change of direction patterns at the young age. As they get older, that would be less beneficial, as they get plenty of that type of work in practice.

4: How to structure workouts for the maximum benefits

Everyone's time is valuable. Whether he's a 5 year old T-Ball player or a 20 year Major League Veteran, there is opportunity cost involved with how they're spending their time. I know for my son, his opportunity cost of going to practice is not playing the Xbox. So with that said, we don't want to waste anyone's valuable time at practice doing a workout that may not be designed well enough to achieve the desired results. To do this, we want to structure our workouts around the most beneficial movements while ensuring we do not take too much time out of the scheduled practice allotment.

For the elementary age player, I generally see practices around the two hour mark. I believe most teams practice 2-3 times a week at most, so that is what I am going to use in this section to design an ideal program. Regardless of the number of days per week, two things should remain constant.

The first is that workouts should be done after a general warmup, but before baseball activities, such as throwing or batting. There are multiple reasons for this, including the benefit of it being additional muscle prep, and getting maximum buy in from players (by doing it at the end, they're already tired and some may have excuses to leave early or skip it). You should not be concerned about the workout tiring the kids out, because any good quality workout designed for strength, speed, or power development should not be exhausting or feel like conditioning. Conditioning is the opposite of what we are focusing on here.

The second constant is that the allotted time for the workout should be no more than 15 minutes. The main focus of going to practice is to play baseball, not to work out. Working out is just a tool we use to develop the components to give our kids the competitive advantage on the field. So while it is obviously important, and is my career, it is obviously not the primary objective of practice. As the kids get older and start playing at the high school level, they will have dedicated strength training sessions with most high level programs. Within those 15 minutes, we need to ensure there is appropriate rest time; as we said, this is not intended to be conditioning work.

It is my professional opinion that the most efficient and effective way to structure a 15 minute youth training block would be to select a few movements and build the workout from there. Assuming you have two practices a week, I would pick 4 movements for each day, and stick with those movements. For example, if practice is every Monday and Thursday, every Monday will have squats, pushups, medicine ball shot puts, and lunges, and every Thursday will have Rear Foot Elevated (RFE) split squats, planks, medicine ball fake scoops, and bird dogs. A sample Linear Progression program would look like this:

MONDAYS

3 sets of each movement

Week 1	Week 2	Week 3	Week 4	Week 5	Week 6
Squatsx10	Squatsx10	Squatsx10	Squatsx8	Squatsx8	Squatsx8
MB Shot Putx6 Each	MB Shot Put x 6 Each	MB Shot Put x 6 Each	MB Shot Put x 6 Each	MB Shot Put x 6 Each	MB Shot Put x 6 Each
Lunges x 6 Each	Lunges x 6 Each	Lunges x 6 Each	Lunges x 4 Each	Lunges x 4 Each	Lunges x 4 Each
Pushups x 5	Pushups x 5	Pushups x 5	Pushups x 8	Pushups x 8	Pushups x 8

THURSDAYS

3 sets of Each Movement

Week 1	Week 2	Week 3	Week 4	Week 5	Week6
RFESS x 5 Each	RFESS x 5 Each	RFESS x 5 Each	RFESS x 3 Each	RFESS x 3 Each	RFESS x3 Each
Plank 30 sec	Plank 30 sec	Plank 30 sec	Plank 30 sec	Plank 30 sec	Plank 30 sec
Fake Scoop x 3 each	Fake Scoop x 3 each	Fake Scoop x 3 each	Fake Scoop x 5 each	Fake Scoop x 5 each	Fake Scoop x 5 each
Bird Dog x 5 each	Bird Dog x 5 each	Bird Dog x 5 each	Bird Dog x 8 each	Bird Dog x 8 each	Bird Dog x 8 each

Add more weight in weeks 4-6 (except MB Shot Put, Pushups, fake scoops, and bird dogs)

This is an example of a linear progression program. The key word there is progression. Notice after the first 3 weeks either the weight or the reps increased. If the weight increases, the reps decrease. If the weight stays the same, then the reps increase. The only exception to this is a plank.

Now, this was a sample 6 week 2 days a week program. I really believe 4 weeks is the minimum number of weeks you need to stick with the same movements, and 4 weeks would be the minimum number of weeks before being able to increase weight or reps for this age group. If I were to write, say a 3 month program, I would probably switch up some of the movements at the month and a half point, while keeping the most important movements the whole time (squat, lunge, RFE SS). I would swap out the other movements for similar stimulus generating movements, such as changing up the starting position for the MB Shot put.

If you have three days a week to practice, then you could add an additional 4 movements from the list I provided earlier in this book.

One more key note is that, breaking the total reps up into smaller sets is shown to be more beneficial when the goal is strength or power, than doing all the reps of one movement and moving on to the next exercise. For example, in Monday's workout we have 30 total squats, 18 MB shot puts on each side, 18 lunges on each side, and 15 pushups on each side. It would probably be faster and easier on the coaches if we did one set of each movement as follows:

Monday: (THIS IS NOT THE SUGGESTED WAY TO DO IT)

One Set of:

Week 1	Week 2	Week 3
Squats x 30	Squats x 30	Squats x 30
MB Shot Put x 18 Each Side	MB Shot Put x 18 Each Side	MB Shot Put x 18 Each Side
Lunges x 18 each side	Lunges x 18 each side	Lunges x 18 each side
Pushups x 15 each side	Pushups x 15 each side	Pushups x 15 each side

However, while this is faster and probably easier for the coaches, and it would be better than not doing any exercises, it is not as effective as breaking the reps into smaller sets. You want to stay within a rep range where the athlete's form and intent do not break down. Remember, at this age, the goal is development!!

So, in conclusion, using the basics of the movements discussed in chapter 2 and not wasting time doing minimal productive exercises as discussed in Chapter 3 will help build the foundation for having a long, healthy athletic career.

Chapter 5: Structuring a Pre-game or Pre-Practice Warm Up

This was not originally going to be a topic in this book, but the more I thought about it, the more I felt it is just as important, if not more important to address a proper practice and game warmup protocol. So many coaches who don't have any formal training revert back to the old school way of stretching prior to playing, and while having the best of intentions, they are actually putting their players at a higher risk of injury. What I am talking about here is the stereotypical static stretches, bend over and touch your toes and hold for 30 seconds, reach your right arm across the body and hold for 30 seconds, etc. Current research has shown that stretching the muscle fibers in this manner before the body is warmed up has the potential to decrease power output and strength of the stretched muscle, and also increases the risk of injury. Therefore, it is imperative to do a dynamic warmup as the first part of your practice or pre-game routine. In this chapter, I will share with you my favorite go to warmup movements, and at the end an example of a pre-game warmup that I have done. By no means is this the ONLY warmup I do; I like to vary the exercises while keeping the same stimulus. We want to prep the body for fast explosive movements, especially in the hamstrings, glutes, abdominals, and rotator cuff muscles.

Moving exercises (5-10 yards each)

High Knees

High Knees are always one of the first warmup exercises I do each day. It is basic movement prep. We want to stimulate blood flow and raise the internal body temperature using basic movement prep exercises.

Butt Kicks

I always do butt kicks after high knees as a basic movement prep.

Side Shuffle

The Side Shuffle is another basic movement prep exercise, but here we start to prepare the body for lateral movements. There are a lot of YouTube videos demonstrating the Side Shuffle exercise.

Karaoke

Karaoke is another basic movement prep exercise, but it is the next step in the progression to prepare the body for lateral movements.

Side Push Offs

Side Push offs prepare the body for producing lateral force (producing force into the ground to propel the body sideways). In baseball, this directly relates to a pitcher pushing off the rubber, or a runner making the initial movement to sprint out of their lead off position as well as the push off portion of an outfielder using a crow hop.

Lunge with twist

The Lunge with twist preps the body for rotational activities such as throwing or batting while also warming up the hip, knee, and ankle joints. The hands make a slightly upwards path during the rotation.

Lunge with Punch

The Lunge with Punch warms up the hip, knee, and ankle joint, while also activating the scaps.

Lunge with Overhead Reach

The Lunge with Punch warms up the shoulder, hip, knee, and ankle joint, while also activating the rotator cuff muscles as well as spine erectors. You want the athlete to reach as high as possible while extending the thoracic part of the spine. A good queue I use with the kids is "big chest and reach high".

Hamstring Scoops

Hamstring Scoops prep the hamstrings for activity.

A-Skips

The purpose of an A-Skip is to drive force hard into the ground to prepare the body for sprinting properly.

Stationary Exercises (5-10 reps each side while standing in place)

Hip Rotation

Hip rotations prepare your body for rotational activities such as throwing and batting.

Hip Full Swings

Full hip swings help prepare for rotational activities using power, such as batting.

90/90 shoulder

90/90 is a highly important movement prep for throwing.

No Money

No Money (internal/external shoulder rotation) is highly important for throwing preparation.

Alternating Arm Swings

This is a simple exercise. Slightly bend the knees, feet hip width apart, bend at the hips, while keeping a flat back. Swing arms back and forth.

Overhead Internal/External Rotation

Reach arms overhead, and rotate at the shoulder to turn the arms palms out and then palms in.

Joint Prep (Controlled Articular Rotations / CARs)

The purpose of CARs is to increase the range of motion of a single joint. Increasing the range of motion will help lower the chances of sustaining an injury.

When performing CARs, it is important to make the entire body as tight and rigid as possible to ensure only the targeted joint is moving. CARs can be done with any joint, but I am just going to cover the joints I see as most important for a youth baseball player. If you have any further questions regarding these joints or other joints, please reach out to me with your questions. You could also search the joint + CARs on YouTube (e.g. "hip CARs" or "ankle Cars") and find several videos on the topic. I would suggest watching one produced by someone with FRC or FRCms in their bio.

When doing CARs exercises, it is important you are working the far end range of motion of the joint. In circular exercises, such as Back CARS or Shoulder CARs, you are trying to make the largest circle you can with that joint. For more stable joints, such as the knee or elbow, we are going to the full end range of the joint. CARs exercises are always performed slowly.

Back CARs

The Back CARs we are going to discuss targets the Thoracic part of the spine. This is a major rotator of the body when doing movements such as throwing a ball or swinging a bat. The Thoracic is the middle portion of the spine. Only that portion should bend, and rotate.

To begin, we will flex at the Thoracic (almost like performing a crunch but standing up), and begin rotating to the left. The left shoulder turns back, and then dips backwards. You rotate around the circle until reaching the starting point. From there you rewind, going back the opposite direction.

Shoulder CARs

This will be the hardest CARs exercise to explain without being there in person or using a video. I strongly encourage you to look at this one on YouTube.

To start, we make the entire body stiff like a statue (queue I use with children). We will start with the right shoulder, so the left hand is in a fist and down to the side next to the left hip. The right arm is also to the side but open palm rotated as far externally (turned out/palm up direction) as possible. Slowly start raising the arm forward while continuing to rotate the palm out externally. The key here is to rotate only at the shoulder, not at the wrist or elbow.

As the arm gets overhead, and slightly past the ear you will encounter a sticking point. Here we internally rotate (at the shoulder) bringing the thumb back around the bottom side of the band and palm facing out again. This allows the arm to continue its large circle.

Continue rotating that palm around so at the bottom of the circle you are almost to a handcuff position. The circle ends at the bottom with the back of your hand touching the right hip.

Now you rewind and go back the way you came. Once you complete this repetition, switch to the left shoulder.

Elbow CARs

Elbow CARs is pretty straight forward. The athlete tucks both elbows into the side of his body. Arms start with the elbows fully extended and the palms facing upwards. Both elbow joints need to be fully rotated externally, meaning the palms should be facing as far outward from the body as possible, while ensuring the wrists are not turning or bending.

Next, as the athlete flexes/bends their elbows, the elbows need to continue turning out as much as possible, until the elbow has fully bent.

At this point, the palms should be near the shoulders. Now, the athlete rotates internally from the elbows so palms now face down, and are still turned as far in that direction as possible.

Knee CARs

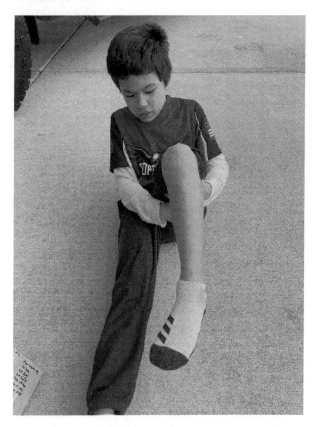

The easiest way to do knee CARs is to start in a seated position. Hold the leg you will be working by placing the hands under the hamstring. This is to help ensure you don't move at the hip. Most people are not aware, but the knee is supposed to be able to slightly rotate. By increasing the knee's rotational range of motion, we hope to reduce the chances of a knee injury such as an ACL tear. From this position, turn at the top of the tibia (shin bone) left and right. You should also not be moving at the ankle. If you are doing it correctly, with a stiff stable ankle, your foot will go left and right. However, this movement needs to be caused by the rotation at the top of the tibia, and not by the ankle moving.

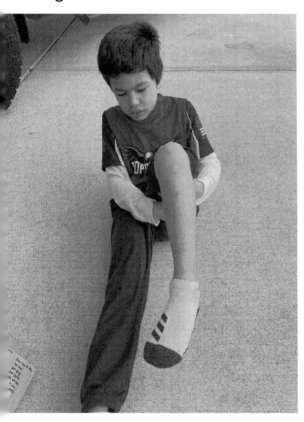

A Sample Pre-Game/Pre-Practice Warm Up

This should only take 10-12 minutes once the kids learn the exercises. Generally, I will set up 3 cones starting at the foul line and going out towards center field 10 yards apart. So we are going 30 yards and turning around, with each exercise moving 10 yards. At each cone, we switch exercises. Some will repeat. For the sake of simplicity, I will leave an empty row after each 30 yard segment.

30 yards	Slow jog
30 yards	Slow back pedal
10 yards	High knees
10 yards	Butt Kicks
10 yards	High knees
10 yards	Butt Kicks
10 yards	High Knees
10 yards	Butt Kicks
30 yards (change direction at each cone)	Side Shuffle
30 yards (change direction at each cone)	Karaoke

10 yards	Side Push Off facing infield
10 yards	Side Push Off facing OF wall
10 yards	Jog it out
10 yards	Lunge with punch
10 yards	Lunge with rotation
10 yards	Lunge with Overhead Reach
10 yards	Reverse lunge w/ punch
10 yards	Reverse lunge w/ punch
10 yards	Reverse lunge w/ OH reach
20 yards	Hamstring Scoops
10 yards	Jog it out
30 yards	A-Skips

Now we either all line up on the foul line, in rows, or circle up. How you decide to organize everyone to do this next part is not important. This is the stationary dynamic warmup.

10 reps (5 each direction)	Hip Rotations
10 Reps (5 each direction)	Hip Swings
10 reps	90/90 shoulders
10 reps	Overhead Internal/external
10 reps (each arm)	Alt arm swings
10 reps	No Money
10 reps	90/90 shoulders
10 reps	Overhead Internal/external
10 reps	Alt arm swings
10 reps	No Money
3 times each direction	Back CARs
2 times each arm	Shoulder CARs
10 times	Elbow CARs
10 times each knee/direction	Knee Cars
10 reps	Squat Jumps

After the stationary dynamic warmup I really like to do something explosive to get them moving fast again. This can be as simple as 2-4 10 yard sprints, or can be some type of agility/reaction drill. One I like to use is to have them lay down face up on the foul line and when I say "go", they react by getting up as fast as they can and sprinting to the first cone at 10 yards. We repeat that a few times and can change their starting position each time. Then it's time to play ball!

Final Thoughts:

I want to stress the importance of anti-rotational movements, such as the MB Fake Scoop. I purposely chose the cover design to include Lee swinging and doing the MB Fake Scoop, because one is an action most youth baseball players do A LOT, while the other is one I have yet to ever see a youth team do. Working on the "deceleration" phase (I put it in quotation marks because in physics, 'deceleration' is not a real term; it is actually called negative acceleration –

but deceleration is the commonly used term) is extremely important if one of your goals is to reduce injury risk.

Think about it like this: If you are building a race car and you only focus on increasing the horsepower to increase the car's acceleration so that you can win the race, but you neglect to also build the breaking system to handle the increase in horsepower, you are probably going to crash. This example is not exactly the same, but it shows how the concept of training deceleration exercises is very important.

The Walton High School Weight Room in Marietta, GA

A common excuse I have heard from youth coaches as to why they do not incorporate strength programs within their practice plans is the lack of equipment or a facility. As you probably noticed in the demonstration pictures from Chapter 2, minimal equipment is needed. Having a weight room set up, similar to the picture above is a nice luxury, but for youth athletes, it is way more than necessary. A few light resistance bands, some light medicine balls, and if you can get them, some light dumbbells or kettlebells is more than enough equipment to do a productive work out on the field. If resources are scarce, I would prioritize resistance bands (they are very inexpensive) and light medicine balls over dumbbells and kettlebells.

Acknowledgements:

I would like to recognize and thank Bryan Eisenberg and Francisco Rivas for helping me with the title and cover of the book, as well as Karen Romano for helping with the proof reading.

Additionally, I want to thank my son Lee for the idea of this book. Without him, this book would have never been written. (He also drove a hard bargain on getting to spend half and save half of the book's royalties). He is the 8 year old in most of the photos and on the cover. His team, the Hopewell Mustangs, won the Dizzy Dean World Series for 7U last year in 2021, and I want to thank his coaches for doing everything the right way! It is stressful being a baseball guy and not being present to help develop my son, but we found an awesome group of coaches to provide that for him.

I want to thank my 5 year old son Alex for being the demonstration model for some of the pictures when Lee was not available to do them.

And lastly, I want to thank the Detroit Tigers for providing me the platform to market this book and get it in the hands of those coaches who can most benefit from it.

NOTES:

Made in the USA
Columbia, SC
31 January 2022

55121712R00061